RAIN, COFFEE, AND YOU

Harold Patrick Mercado

Edited by Marigold Uy

Philippine Copyright

by GMGA Publishing

September 2020

ISBN:

Praises for

RAIN, COFFEE, AND YOU

"I loved how this book gave me a glimpse of my yesterday's heartbreaks and made me reminisce the past all of a sudden."

—Nicole Pidlaoan, Campus Journalist

"Love is all what it takes. This book is indeed interesting! The author used simple words, but he was able to convey extreme emotions. The story beyond each piece is vivid—a thing that you'll surely love. I found love and heartache in each page. I can say that this is a craft made with heart and utmost passion."

—John Paul De Guzman, Writer

"There's nothing more comforting than sipping a cup of coffee and indulging yourself with a book while listening to the music of rain splattering against your windowpane. This compilation of relatable love poems and verses will make you reminisce about the good old times with someone you loved. Rain, Coffee, and You presents nostalgic thoughts of selfless love and heartbreaks—perfect for someone who loves being senti-motional on rainy days."

—**Mary Jane Iglesias**, former editor-in-chief of The Forum

"The colors of words made me feel a sudden mix of emotions. The metaphors satisfied my needs to realize what it takes to love someone. This book reminds me to love again and to take the risk of giving your heart away. This is best with a cup of coffee on rainy days."

—**Earl Joseph Salapantan**, Writer and Campus Journalist

"I had mixed emotions after reading this book, because I can somehow relate to the message it conveys. When I started reading, there's something I can't control. And it's the pain I feel that's getting on my nerves as I read every single word written in this book. I can sense the author's emotion while reading this book; he is one of those people who used to keep the pain he has been feeling silently. If you want to be hurt and to bring out all the hidden pain you've been feeling, maybe this book is best for you."

—**Chrisel Villafranca**, Artist

FOREWORD

When songs are at their sweetest, that is when they hold the most painful memories.

At a young age, poetry reading and poetry writing became spellbinding activities for me. It was that grandeur of innocent love on verses, on words, on melody, and on flowing-free patterns which provides that inner calm to dance with the flamingos and soar like an eagle.

It was magnificent. Writing shall always be magnificent.

Now at 44, a collection of thoughts, of emotions, of verses came by me. One authored by a former student, this masterpiece, in its mighty magical secretive way, narrates a love story that seems so familiar, really familiar. And while going through every detail of it, I realized how unexpected and odd it was that this collection of verses— this collection of thoughts and emotions—has brought to memory once again a love story in my own time—barely 28 years ago!

This, dear readers, is the magic of words. This is the art of writing.

The beauty of any literary piece lies in multiple aspects. The art in writing delves on various factors.

Read on and discover both the beauty and the art.

—WINLOVE PALACIO MENDOZA

ACKNOWLEDGEMENT

My completion of this book could not have been accomplished without the guidance of my agent and mentor, Ms. Ayo Gutierrez. Thank you for guiding me throughout this success.

Also, I offer my gratitude and respect to my former teacher and adviser, Mr. Winlove Palacio Mendoza, for saying 'yes' right away when I asked him to write the foreword of this book. You will always be the one I look up to.

I cannot express my enough thanks to my family for their continued love and support: Leonardo Mercado, my father; Martina Mercado, my mother; Helen Rufo, Hilda Mercado, Hailyn Hermono, Henalyn Garcia, Hipolita Baldinar, and Marife Mercado, my sisters; Leonardo Mercado, Jr., my brother; Rolenjoy Rufo, Ma. Jamaica Hermono, Raine Abbey Rufo, and Mary Rohilyn Baldinar, my nieces. I offer my sincere appreciation for all the things you have done for me.

To you, who broke my heart, thank you. I thank you for helping me learn what it takes to love someone.

Finally, I want to thank God for always making everything possible.

To you,

who broke my heart,

I want you to know

that I will always remember you

as the person

who taught me a lesson.

Lie

I am now happy

I'm not affected by you

It is just a *lie*.

Moon

When I see the moon,

it just reminds me of you—

so near, yet so far.

And Here I am Again

I promise I'll return.

And here I am again, drowning in your words.

I feel like my heart skips a beat every time I try to send you messages.

I feel like I can't breathe every time I wait for your replies.

And here I am again, hoping that your words would ease all my pain.

I feel like I'm trapped in your warmth, with your love.

I can't breathe. I feel like I'm drowning in my tears.

And here I am again, thinking you will not leave again.

Please stay.

I Still Remember

I still remember the warmth of your hand when you held mine as we walked at the street under the rain.

You've mastered the art of holding on to me when it rains.

I still remember the feeling of being safe in your arms when you hugged and kissed me.

You've mastered the art of hugs and kisses.

I still remember the sweet sound of your giggles when you brushed my hair up, and tried to get me pissed off.

You were really expert in doing that thing.

I still remember the cutest way of you eating your favorite ice cream, and putting some on my face when you noticed that I was staring at you the whole time.

You were really expert in doing that thing.

I still smell the fragrance of your fresh and natural breath when you whispered in my ear on the Sunday morning.

You were really expert in doing that thing.

I still remember how crazy I was when I was with you. The way you dressed your hair, your beautiful face, your innocent look, and your natural you.

You were perfect in my eyes.

I still remember how I realized that you were really the one destined to be with me for the rest of my life. You've made me realized that we belong together when you told me that it was okay to be not okay and when you insisted that we were really meant to be, because you were crazy and I was out of my mind.

You were a kind of paradox.

I still remember my heart thundering at the thought of your smile.

You've mastered the art of moving ever so slowly when you walked with that wavy hair bouncing up and down and with that magnetic look of your eyes that captured everything they reached.

But most of all...

I still remember how fast things went off.

I still remember how you've changed.

I still remember how your hands loosened their firm hold on mine and totally slipped away.

I still remember how your kiss marks faded on my cheeks.

I still remember how hurt I was when you turned your back on me, instead of hugging me.

I still remember how you closed your eyes when you did not want to see me anymore.

I still remember how your meaningful smiles became the meaningless ones.

I still remember how fast it changed, it faded, and it evaporated—everything!

I still remember how my world collapsed when you left me alone here.

You promised me that you would stay, but you broke not only your promises but also my heart—into a million of pieces.

Now there is only one thing I could say:

You've mastered the art of breaking my heart.

Once Together

Only you and me

We two were once together

Now we are strangers.

My Star

Do you remember the night we were looking at the stars?

I remember the night we spent gazing at the stars, when you were still mine. How happy we were, sitting on the grass, the wind on our faces.

We were happy and contented sitting there at that park where we used to be, while looking at the beautiful view above with smiles on our lips.

You sighed, and I knew something bothered you.

"You said before that I was your star, didn't you?" You looked at me in the eyes.

I did tell you that. You're the star that I adore, the only one that mattered among million others in the sky.

"Yes, I did. Why?"

You turned away, and I see you hesitating.

You looked up at the sky again. Your voice was quite sad. "What if I lose my light? What if I'm no longer pretty?"

I held your face, so we could gaze at each other's eyes. I looked at your teary eyes. I saw a little bit apprehension in them.

"When I said I love you, it's because you were so far, like a star I couldn't reach, but your light reached me. I didn't mean that it was the only reason why I fell for you. I want you to know that I love you for who you are. I will still love you even if you don't spark like a star in the night. I will continue loving you even if you don't give light in my darkest night. I will love you still even if you are not beautiful."

By then, tears rolled down your cheeks and I wiped them away with my fingers.

I kissed your forehead, not wanting to see you cry. If anything, I only want you to be happy.

I slowly removed my lips from your forehead. Then, I hugged you tightly. I wanted to give you the assurance that you wanted, that you deserved.

"I love you, whatever it takes."

Crush

I wake up every morning

My eyes want to see you every day

You make my life interesting

It's all I want to say.

When I see you I want to shine bright

Enough for you to see and notice me

That I can also be your light

You're my idol, and you'll always be.

I admire you a lot

You inspire me to be my best

Do I tell it to you or not?

My heart thunders inside my chest.

I Waited for You

On the day you left, you promised we'd meet again, in the place where we used to gaze at the stars.

Days, weeks, months, even years had passed, but you didn't come back. Morning came each time, but nothing stayed the same.

I try to look for you, with hopes that you're in our rendezvous point, waiting for me.

Yet I was the one who waited there, ignoring the cold breeze, the sympathetic stares of people who thought I was wasting my time.

All these years, I waited, just in case, even when I knew you wouldn't return.

I returned one night, promised myself this will be the last that I will hope.

"Please wait for me." I heard your voice. I saw an image of you, on the day you said goodbye.

I wanted to embrace you, to believe that what I see was real. But you weren't there after all. I stood, frozen.

Tears rolled down my cheeks. The realization dawned on me. Your image was just a product of my imagination, of my despair, and of my longing for you.

I wanted to scream, but I couldn't find my voice. My knees felt weak. My body trembled with emotion.

You left with a promise, and I held on to your words with each day that passed.

I will never wait for you anymore.

It could have been better for you to have left without a word, than to have given me a false hope.

It would have been better to have made me believe that you loved me, even if it's a lie.

More Than Words

I want you to know

how I love you so;

You're like a starlight

that twinkles in the night.

Depend on me, I'm your hero

I'll save you from any foe

Your hugs and kisses are all that I desire

You light up my heart's fire.

Lean on me as we gaze at the sky

I promise you my love, 'til the day I die

I will love you forever and always

I will prove to you in so many ways.

My love for you is more than words

for you are my whole world;

I will do anything for you

So promise me, that you'll love me too

24

Forgive Me

I looked at myself in the mirror. I could still see you beside me. I don't think you can see the 'love' in the mirror.

Forgive me for still thinking of you, and I will forgive you for already forgetting about me.

Forgive me for still wishing to hold your hand, and I will forgive you for letting go of mine.

Forgive me for still keeping our pictures, and I will forgive you for burning them already.

Forgive me for still sending you messages, and I will forgive you for ignoring them every single time.

Forgive me for still returning to our favorite places, and I will forgive you for leaving me alone.

Forgive me for smiling every time I see you, and I will forgive you for choosing not to look at me.

Forgive me for still crying, and I will forgive you for laughing with somebody else now.

Forgive me for still choosing to love you, and I will forgive you for giving up on me.

Forgive me for still waiting, and I will forgive you for leaving.

Forgive me for still holding on, and I will forgive you for already moving on.

Time to Say Goodbye

I didn't wish for this to end this way,

but I've decided this from the very first day;

I chose to grow and be free—

to become a better version of me.

I apologize for being selfish,

but this is my only wish;

It's time for us to part,

even if it breaks your heart.

It's time to say goodbye

Forgive me for choosing to cry

I know everything will be okay,

even when you're far away.

Everything's Changed

Everyone I know said I've changed.

I am not the person I used to be before.

It started when you left.

Everything felt so right before. I was happy, and you were contented.

We used to be so happy. My smile used to reach my eyes.

I used to be so positive. I look forward to mornings because you were there to remind me that there's always something I can look forward to. Maybe because I looked forward to seeing you every single day.

Everything used to be so bright.

...until you left me hanging. You ended what we had without telling me why. I wanted to know what I did, but you never told me your reason for leaving. And I cling to our memories, trying to find what went wrong but I just couldn't...

We used to be so perfect.

What went wrong? What changed?

Everything.

I Find It Odd

I find it odd—

Because I did everything,

but it wasn't enough for you

I have everything,

but I feel nothing

We are so near,

yet so far.

I find it odd—

I gave you everything

in exchange for nothing

All I gave you was my love,

but I got pain in return

I may look whole

but inside, I am broken.

I find it odd—

I'm tired,

but I'm still trying

You say that you love me,

but you aren't giving me enough proof

I am still thinking of you,

but all you did was leave.

I find it odd—

Because you're asking me to forgive you,

even when you haven't changed

I have to move on,

but you make it hard for me to do so

Because even then,

it's still easier said than done.

I find it odd—

Your love makes me happy,

even with all the pain and tears

I need to forget about you,

but I can't get you out of my mind

Because I know you already love someone
else,

yet here I am, still in love with you.

I find it odd—

Because I smile in front of other people,

but I cry when I'm alone

Because even when I want to love someone
else,

but my heart only wants you

Because I thought I can make you stay,

but I was wrong all along.

I Miss You

Missing you is like taking my breath away. It feels heavy on my chest. And it is impossible to survive.

I miss your touch. I miss those moments that you held my hands. It felt like warming my soul.

I miss how you hugged me when I felt cold. You were really good at making me feel better every time I was having a bad day.

I miss you whispering in my ear every morning. Your kisses were enough to get me going every day.

I miss your voice saying how much you loved me and how willing you were to be with me for the rest of your life. Your voice never failed to make my heart beat so fast as if it was in a race.

I miss seeing how you control your laughter when I tell you jokes. You were so beautiful that I could help kissed you. I just couldn't resist the urge to feel your lips in mine.

Most of all, I miss you. I am still missing you. I know a long time has already passed, but I just can't let go of something that made me feel happy and special. I found myself with you, but you found yours with somebody else.

It was never a waste of time to be with you, because I wanted to be with you every moment of my life. If only I could tie myself to you, I did. But I couldn't do that. I couldn't be that selfish. I didn't want to force myself to you when I know you're not going to be happy with me.

I want to say sorry if I am still stuck on the past. I know that you loved me, because I felt that. But maybe, love isn't really enough to make someone stay.

You said that you wanted to find yourself, so I let you go. I wanted you to be at your best. But while you were searching, you found someone that matched you better.

Now, I can't help myself but think of you. They say that if you always think of someone, maybe that person thinks of you often, too. But I wonder if you really do.

I want to ask you in person if you still think of me the way that I think of you, but I end up missing you more than ever.

Pillow

Only my pillow knows

how many nights I've cried;

Only my pillow knows

how I cry every night thinking of you.

I Can't

Yes, loving can hurt. Love can make us feel complete, but it can also make us feel broken.

Yes, we used to be together. We spent the hours with each other before. And no, I can't just forget about our past.

Yes, we used to hold each other's hands while we walked in the street as the sun sets. And no, I can't just forget about that.

Yes, you used to brush your lips on mine while tears were falling down my cheeks—to remind me that everything will be all right. And no, I can't just forget about that.

Yes, I used to lean my head on your shoulder every night while we were looking at the stars. I loved the way your breath tickled my forehead. And no, I can't just forget about that.

Yes, I used to wrap you in my arms when the cold breeze came our way, and you used to hug me back. You made me feel your warmth, your care, and your love. And no, I can't just forget about it.

Yes, I used to place your head on my chest while we lie on the grass of that park where we used to go to, and you used to love hearing the beats of my heart which, you said, sounded music to your ears. And no, I can't just forget about that.

Yes, we used to find time for each other—no matter how busy we were with our own lives, and we were determined to make our relationship grow ever since. And no, I can't just forget about that.

Yes, we used to fight for our love against the people around us and against the world. We used to swim in the deepest sea, climb the highest hills, and take every challenge that hindered us from reaching each other. And no, I can't just forget about that.

But, everything went as fast as the light flashed.

Yes, we really loved each other, yet it was not still enough. And no, I was not the one who left.

You.

Gave.

Up.

And no, I couldn't do anything about it.

When you left, you heard no words from me.

I just let you say that you were not happy with me anymore, with what was happening, and with us.

I just let you pull away when I tried to kiss you.

I just let you slip your hands away from mine.

I just let you turn your back on me.

In other words, I just let you free.

But I couldn't just forget about how happy and contented we were before.

And until now, I can't just forget about you.

Waiting

This is a world

where nothing is constant;

People wait for someone to arrive,

while waiting for someone else to leave.

What If

Every morning when I wake up, I look at your face as you sleep. You look so innocent that I can't resist taking this sight all in. I would not mind looking at you the whole day. That's how much I love you.

I trace your features: your brows, your lids, your small nose, and your sweet red lips.

I smile at the sound you make.

Then, I stop. Something pops on my mind.

We're together. You're mine.

But, what if...

What if one morning, you'll wake up and realize that something's wrong, something's missing, and something's not supposed to be?

What if I could no longer make you happy with my jokes?

What if one day, you'll realize that you aren't comfortable with me anymore?

What if my kisses no longer make you blush?

What if my hugs are not as warm as it used to be?

What if I can no longer satisfy you with my love?

What if one day, you'll wake up, only to find out that you do not feel the same way?

What if one day, you'll realize that your love for me is fading?

What if you'll feel that I am not enough and that I am not worth all your love?

What if...

What if you choose to leave?

What if you find what's missing in me from another person?

What if you choose to love someone else?

I may not be perfect, but please stay. I am not that sweet or showy. I seldom say 'I love you', but please remember:

I will always choose to stay by your side no matter what happens, because I love you.

And I hope that it is enough reason for you to stay. Because thinking of you leaving me alone makes me insane.

Come Back

It's hard to come back

when you're not there anymore;

It's hard to come back

when I actually didn't leave.

How Can I?

How can I forget someone that made me feel so special?

How can I bury the memories that brought so much happiness and color to my lonely and plain life?

How can I get over of the warmth of your embrace, those that made me feel secured and protected?

How can I erase the feeling of heaven when your lips are pressed against mine?

How can I forget the funny expressions you put on when you tell me jokes?

How can I leave behind the once-sweet words you used to whisper in my ears?

How can I avoid the image of your beautiful face that always enter my mind every now and then?

How can I forget the precious moments we had together?

How can I move on from our past that keeps on pulling me back?

How can I escape from the pain you caused me when you said that what happened between us was just a product of your boredom?

How can I get over the fact that you treated me like an object to pass your time?

How can I forget the love that I have for you when you can't even love me back?

To Feel You Again

I want to feel you again

      your warmth

      your hugs

      your kisses

      your touch to ease away the pain.

Fireworks

You were once my inspiration.

I was lost in the dark, but you lighted up my way.

You brought color in my life that really made it enjoyable to live in.

You let me see happiness in every little thing that happened, so I never felt lonely.

You gave me motivation to open my eyes and wake up every morning to face the world.

You were one of the reasons why I was always looking forward to watch the beautiful sunrise and start the day with a smile.

You were able to make me laugh so loud as if no one was around, because you kept on telling me that I was cute that way.

You added sounds to my quiet world and made me realize that music was an escape from all the struggles in everyday life.

Those were only some of the things that I loved about you.

You were like a firework display at night. You suddenly came into my life.

I was looking for something all my life before, until you came and filled in the missing piece of my heart.

You made me feel special.

You made me feel complete.

You made me feel enough and worth it.

But just as fireworks are, you faded after you made me happy.

You were once my inspiration—my source of happiness and strength.

Now that you are gone, I don't know why I still stand in the place where we watched the fireworks—the exact same place where you left me alone.

Reasons

You can make me smile

without any reason,

but

you can make me cry

with plenty of reasons.

In Theory

In theory, acrophobia isn't really being afraid of heights. Rather, it is the fear of falling.

In the case of nyctophobia, it isn't really being afraid of the dark. Rather, it is the fear of what's in it.

We are not afraid of *something*. We are afraid of what's behind this 'something' and what it may bring to us.

Just like what I've experienced.

I was not afraid of you. Nor I was afraid of falling in love.

I was actually afraid of the pain I might feel in case you already loved someone.

But I still took the risk. I loved you. You were all that mattered to me.

So, I guess we are not really afraid of love. We are afraid of the possibility that the one we love may not love us back.

It hurt when I saw you kissing someone else's lips under that lamppost in that street on that Saturday night.

Behind the two of you kissing was me crying in silence.

49

My Favorite Music

You are my favorite music

Sometimes, you make me happy

Sometimes, you make me sad

But like my favorite music,

you know how to break my heart

With your sharp words and lonely melody,

you always make me hurt.

I Wish I Know

It's hard to move on without knowing the reason why something ended. It's like walking with no direction.

I keep on repeating the same process, retracing the same path, and reimagining the same memories—but I still feel uncertain.

I keep on repeating, retracing, and reimagining.

Maybe when I find out the reason you left, can I finally let go and move on.

I wish I know your reasons. I want to hear your explanation. I want to erase the questions in my head.

I wish I know your reasons. I want to know how your love ebbed. I want to know how it started to fade away.

I wish I know your reasons. I want to ask where I went wrong. I want to know what made you change your mind.

I wish I know your reasons. I want to know why you left me. I want to know if you love someone else already.

I wish I know your reasons. I want to know
what you saw in him that wasn't in me.

52

I'm Tired

I'm tired

to be the one saying "I'm just here"

in a world of

saying "I don't need you."

Memories

If there's one thing I could never forget, it's our memories. They say that if something makes a person happy, they will have a difficult time forgetting it.

I think that explains my pain.

It is not you that I miss; it's the memories. But memories bring back the past. And the past brings back you.

Busy Chasing You

I was busy chasing you

that I've lost my way back home;

I was busy chasing you

that I've forgotten I am breaking.

Even More

The night before we decided to break up, I asked you a question:

"Did you ever love me?"

You were silent. It was obvious that you didn't know what to say. In your hesitance, I found the answer. My heart was like repeatedly being stabbed by a sharp knife in that moment.

"Did you ever love me?" I repeated, my voice quiet.

"I don't know." You started crying.

I thought I was hurt enough, but your answer hurt me even more.

My question was answerable by yes or no. You should have said 'no.' You shouldn't give me hope.

Please, don't give me something to hold on to without any assurance.

It hurts even more to hope on something that will never come true again.

Met and Lost

When I met you,

my world started to spin.

When I lost you,

my world ended its turn.

Always and Never

You will *always* have my heart, no matter what happens. The day my eyes met yours, I have already given it to you—or you have taken it from me.

In contrary, your heart already belongs to someone else. And I know that I will *never* have it for myself, no matter what happens.

Sometimes I Wonder

Sometimes I wonder

if you ever planned our future

when you knew nothing's for sure.

Sometimes I wonder

if you still look back to our past

when you realize time's really going fast.

Sometimes I wonder

if our memories flash in your mind

when you close your eyes.

Sometimes I wonder

if you still think of me

when you drink your coffee.

Sometimes I wonder

if you ever regret our split yesterday,

if you ever imagine what we could have been today.

Every Day

I will choose you, and I will keep choosing you every day. There are so many people in the world, but nothing can be as perfect as you in my eyes.

I will love you, and I will keep loving you every day. My heart beats so fast because of you. You can hear it for yourself. Every beat of it shouts your name.

I will choose to love you, and I will keep choosing to love you—even if you choose to love someone else, and you keep on choosing to love that person until the end.

Rain

Every raindrop

is like my tears,

falling hard

when it's already too heavy.

My Strength

There are mornings when I don't want to open my eyes, even when I am already awake. I want you to be the first thing I see in the morning when I wake up, because you give me strength to face the world.

Now, I can only see you in my dreams. I don't want to wake up if I'm going to lose you the moment I open my eyes. I don't have that enough strength alone. I need you to guide me in my life.

Someone

Someone hugged you

Someone said "I love you"

You replied with "I love you, too."

But that someone isn't me

And there's nothing I can do

but to hide and cry in silence.

If It's Not You

Have you ever stared at a door, waiting for it to open and expecting someone to arrive? I do.

I knew that when you walked out that door, I can't have you anymore. But I still hope that you change your mind.

Until now, I'm not opening that same door—if it's not going to be you.

Shadow

I'm just a shadow

that watches you from behind

and never leaves you.

How I Write Poetry

I need three things to write poetry:
endless rain, a cup of coffee, and you
—inside my head.

Taste Like You

With every sip of my coffee

I remember what we used to be,

because every drop of it

tastes like you.

Letters

I still have the letters you have written for me. I didn't burn them, and I do not have any plan to do so. These hold our memories. Written in them are the things we share and things we hold so dear, when we were still together.

It hurts me to think that you still write letters until now—not for me, but for someone else.

Stars in the Dark

In my hardest and darkest day

with you here, I can never go astray

You always guide me on the right way

with your light as bright as day.

My nights are not melancholic

You are so innocent and angelic

I'm not alone, you want to know why?

You're always there in my own sky.

My life is worth living

because you're there, twinkling

You are my stars at night,

the only one I see, the only one that's bright.

I'm Jealous

I'm jealous of the way you are happy without me. I want to know how you do it.

You can still smile genuinely. You can still act the way you used to do.

You can still face the world and live your life.

You can still look at my eyes when we cross our paths.

Like normal.

Like nothing happened between us.

Like you have never lost me.

Valuing You

You are what I need

You are always willing

to guide and bring out the best in me

I can't live without you, indeed.

The joy you bring is so priceless

I'm happy to have adored you

My life is colorful; I'm not bored

This journey of mine is not useless.

I value you being here

You always go with me anywhere.

To You, Who Broke My Heart

It's been a long time since you broke my heart. I still remember how happy and contented we were before. Every time our memories flash in my mind, it still hurts, that I cry.

I admit that I still love you, but I know we are already over. Someday, it will no longer matter when our eyes meet. To you, who broke my heart, I promise that I will be happy—even without you.

I Believe

You can't force everyone to believe you
but I always do.
I believe that you love me, too
even if it is not true.

It Hurts

It hurts to see you are slowly losing your interest in me. It's like being in a party where you are not invited in the first place.

We are always together, this is true. You are by my side when we walk on the street. You sit with me by the grass while you listen to music on your earphones. You lean your head on my shoulder as we gaze at the stars.

But it feels like you are the moon that I can't reach.

I know something is bothering you. I want to know what it is, but I don't have the courage to ask you.

It hurts!

The pain feels like a knife in my chest. The thought of you gone makes it hard for me to breathe.

I have never prepared myself for this, because I thought we will never reach this point. I believed that our love will last a lifetime.

But here are we now, still as the darkness around us.

"I can't feel it," you said, breaking the long silence.

I almost forgot to breathe for a few seconds when I heard your cold voice.

You can't feel it? But I can. I can feel my heart pounding. I can feel my hands shaking. I can feel my tears blurring my eyes. What can't you feel?

"I can't feel the love anymore," you continued.

I feel my tears rolling down my cheeks. I leaned up and faced you. When I gazed into your eyes, I can't feel any emotion in them.

I have a lot to ask you, but I can't find my voice. I want to beg you to take back what you said, but I can't utter a single word.

"I'm sorry," you said, after a moment.

You stood. I want to stop you from leaving, but I can't move my feet. My knees were shaking.

You glared at me before turning to leave. You walked away, and I can't do anything but watch.

When you were finally gone, I called out your name. I feel like my heart is being torn apart.

I fell on my knees and held my chest. It hurts.

If You Want Love

If he ever hurt you,

remember that I'm here

for you to return to.

If you want love,

you don't have to ask for it

I'll give it to you.

Clock

Have you ever stared at the clock for a
few minutes wishing time would stop? I do.
I do it every time I'm with you.

Someday

Someday I'll meet you

and look straight into your eyes

and ask, "How are you?"

You'll reply, "I'm fine. And you?"

"I'm great, too," I'll say

with a smile.

It's hard to pretend

acting like you're not hurt

but it's the best thing I can do.

Book

I am still reading the book you gave me. I turned the pages, and saw a note in the last page.

It says: "Keep this book, and remember that I will always stay with you, no matter how hard our situation will be. I'll never leave you, I promise."

A tear rolled down my cheek, because you failed to keep your promise.

Everything

I'm trying to forget you

but when I close my eyes,

even the darkness reminds me of you.

I think I know why—

because you used to be

my everything.

My Dream

Before, it looked like my dream was so far
away and impossible to achieve. But you
came into my life and my dream came true.

What Does It Feel?

What does it feel

to leave someone who loves you?

What does it feel

to break my heart into pieces?

What does it feel

to walk away from our favorite place?

What does it feel

to be with someone new?

Heaven

When I was a child, I have always wondered how it feels to be in heaven. Now that I have you in my arms, I already know what it feels like.

Our Song

We wrote our song together

but only I did perform it.

We planned our future together

but only I did accomplish it.

We promised to last forever

but only I did stay.

Nightmare

There are things I wish I have never seen. There are events I wish have never happened. There are people I wish I have never met. Because all those things that I have seen, events that have happened, and people that I met are like wounds. They have healed; but they left scars—those that will haunt me in my sleep.

Clauses

I am your dependent clause,

and you are my independent clause.

You can be complete without me,

while I'm incomplete without you.

Ironic

I'm yours,

but you did not lose me.

You're not mine,

but I've lost you.

A Piece of Cake

Loving you is like a piece of cake. It's very easy to fall for you. I have never expected that I would be writing poetry for someone. You were just a simple person, but that made you more special. There's so much to write about you.

Getting my complete attention is just a piece of cake for you. You don't have to sing or dance. Your smile alone can melt my heart, and makes me smile in return.

But you know what? Breaking my heart is also a piece of cake for you. Just by ignoring me and pretending that you don't know me at all, you can make me feel the pain—like taking my heart out of my chest and slicing it into pieces.

And just by forgetting our memories together and making me feel like I did not take up any space in your heart, you can make my tears fall—like a piece of cake.

Happy Ending

I was once fond of happy endings. But when I finished the last book you gave me, I asked you, "Why did you buy me a sad-ending story this time?"

You smiled. There was a hidden message in your eyes, one that I couldn't discern.

"Every story that ends with 'And they live happily ever after' starts with 'Once upon a time'. But not all stories starting with 'Once upon a time' end with 'And they live happily ever after,'" you answered.

I didn't know why you told me that. But now, I guess I already know why.

Maybe you were just trying to make me love stories with sad endings.

Maybe you were just preparing me for the sad ending of our own story.

Maybe you were just trying to make it easy for me to accept that we would not have a happy ending.

Love Story

I don't want to read

other romance books;

I just want to have

our own love story.

Sun and Moon

I am the sun, and you are the moon. I am willing to set and give up my spot, for you to rise up in the sky.

Sadly, we will never have the chance to rule the sky together.

The Love of my Life

"There are so many fish in the sea," my friends keep on saying when you left.

I stared at them for a few seconds before shrugging my shoulders.

"But she's just not any fish. She's the love of my life.

You're Still the One

You're still the one

who makes me smile,

even if you're not around.

You're still the one

who occupies my mind,

think of no one else but you.

You're still the one

who gives me warmth when I'm cold

just by imagining you hugging me.

You're still the one

who makes my heart beat so fast

when I think of your kisses.

You're still the one

I am dreaming of until now,

even if I am awake.

You're still the one
who keeps me hoping for something
that is impossible to happen.

You're still the one
that I choose and I will keep choosing,
even if you've already chosen him.

You're still the one
who makes my tears fall down
every night I miss you.

You're still the one
who hurts me so bad
every time I see you with him.

Compass

Without you by my side is like being in a wild jungle. There are so many trees. Everything seems to be the same. I don't know where to go—which direction to take.

I need you, my compass. I need you to know where is the north, south, west, and east. I need you to show me where the right direction is—the right path towards you.

I am Willing

I am willing

to let you go,

even if it means

finding happiness with someone else.

I am willing

to let you go,

even if it means

drowning myself in tears.

I am willing

to let you go,

even if it means

being in a never-ending darkness.

I am willing

to let you go,

even if it means

breaking my heart.

I am willing

to let you go,

even if it means

taking my life away.

I Would Rather

I would rather have you as we go against the waves, than to walk alone on the seashore.

I would rather be with you in a battle, than live alone in peace.

I would rather be with you in hard times, than to experience life without love.

I would rather be cursed by the whole universe, than to be hated by you.

I would rather cry with you, than to laugh with someone else.

Do you know why?

I would rather everything be about you, than nothing at all.

Time

It's okay not to be okay

You don't need to force a smile

just to show everybody

that you're not hurting.

It's fine to cry out loud

when you are in pain

There's no reason not to cry

when you actually have every reason for it.

I know it's hard

but you can take your time

Take all the time that you need

for you to heal.

You

I don't believe when they say we cannot sleep because we think too much about too many things. I can't sleep even even if I only think of one thing—you.

Bookmark

There is a part of a book

that I keep on rereading

—in the middle, where the climax is.

Even though I've read it too many times

I keep on returning to that page

because it's my favorite part.

I bookmark that page,

unable to move on to the next

because I don't want to end its story yet.

Silence

I used to love our silence, because I get the chance to hear how your heart beats for me. But now I'm starting to hate it, because it only reminds me of how you left me in silence.

Love is Like a Game

Love is like a game

where the winners really gain

and the losers learn.

Prayer

I want you to know that you are always included in my prayers. I always pray that wherever you are and whoever you are with, you will be forever happy.

I hope that he takes good care of you the way I want you to be taken care of, that he loves you the way I want you to be loved, and that he gives you enough reasons to enjoy life the way I want you to.

I hope that he's already the one for you, so that you will not be hurt again. I hope that he will not leave you, so that you will not be alone ever again.

I always pray for you—not to be mine anymore—but to have the best life you could ever have.

Goldfish

Goldfish in an aquarium

looks cute and happy in your eyes

but you don't know how it feels.

You don't have any idea how hard it could
be

to be in a situation where you can't do
anything

but to get used of it.

Notebook

While I was cleaning my room, I found an old notebook under my bed. It was the notebook I was looking for a long time ago, but when I bought a new one, I forgot about it.

I turned its pages to know its contents. I browsed it and realized that it contained poetry and other writing from when I was broken. And from that moment, I realized how important it was during my healing process.

There are things that played a vital role in our lives, but they are taken for granted when we find a new replacement.

There are things that we ignore at first, only to find value in them when we need them the most.

Coffee

Others put too much sugar

that it doesn't even taste like coffee

I like it just the way it is—

plain, bitter, and dark.

Love is Not Blind

I don't believe every time they say love is

blind. I always see you even if

I close my eyes.

Journey

It doesn't matter

where you are going.

What matters is

who you are going with.

It's Never Easy

This is far from what I've pictured us to be. It's never easy to let you go. Without you in my life is like having a big hole in my heart—waiting to be filled in.

I want to grow old with you. Until our hair becomes grey. Until wrinkles dominate our skin all over the body. Until we can't stand straight. Until our vision becomes blur. Until we can't barely hear what each other says. Until our bones go weak. Until we walk slower than an infant learning to walk.

I want to spend the rest of my life in your arms. To go out on a date every weekend, or watch a romantic movie. To reminisce how we first met and how we ended up together. To visit the park that used to be our meeting place. It's the same park where we became a couple.

I want to be in love with you all over again. If you're going to look in my eyes, you will see how they long for you, how they want to spend the whole day staring at you, and how they can't get enough of you.

But all of these are just my dream. I can't have you anymore.

You asked me to give up, but I can't. I still said I will.

You asked me to stop, but I can't. I still said I will.

You asked me to let you go, but I can't. I still said I will.

If there is one thing I want, it's your happiness. I said I will let you go because I want you to be happy—even if that happiness is not with me. I don't want to be the cause of your misery. I don't want to lock you up in a room with me, when you prefer to be free with him.

But I never thought that letting you go could be this hard. I thought time could heal everything. I thought if I could find someone new, I could finally forget about you. I thought that after all these years, I could finally smile genuinely when I see you with him. But I was wrong.

It's never easy letting you go. It did not end when I let you walk out the door or when I finally told myself that we're over. It will only end if I can accept when I see you happy with him.

But trying to be happy for you feels like torture.

It's either I learn to live with this never-ending process or I'll just have to get used to missing you every day.

I Wish

I wish that

I have enough reasons

to make you stay.

I wish that

I was him

so you won't go away.

My Whole Life

You are not just a single poem; you are
every poem that I write. You are not only a
page of a book; you are the whole book I
make. You are not just a part of my life;
you are my whole life.

There Will Be a Time

There will be a time

there will never be a time

for the two of us.

Destiny

It wasn't easy. Time has passed by. I've moved forward—but I did not forget. I haven't stopped loving you. My love for you did not fade. Nor did it change.

I became what we both dreamed of before. I lived my life as you wanted me to. It was hard. Time just seemed to run slow. It seemed like every night would last forever. Even if I kept myself busy, I couldn't help thinking of you every time I paused a moment.

It seemed impossible for a long time. I still feel the same emotions. I can still smell your scent on my couch. I still see you lying on my bed. I still feel your breath on my neck. I can still remember your lips on mine.

But destiny had other plans. We had to go on our separate ways. You found him on your way, but I treaded my path alone. There was nothing I can do but continue. The world kept on turning and things kept on moving. You were finally moving on. And I could not allow myself to stay stuck forever.

We were destined to meet each other and
be together, but we were not destined to last
forever.

Just a Memory

It's ironic

how the person

who gave you the best memories

ended up being just a memory.

Thank You

Thank you for helping me learn what it
really means to commit to someone, and
what it really takes to do so.

I Don't Have Time

Love me

because I don't have time.

I don't have time

to leave you;

I don't have time

to hurt you.

I don't have time

to be angry with you;

I don't have time

to forget about you.

I don't have time

to break my promises;

I don't have time

to find someone new.

Yesterday, Today, and Someday

There are memories that we always look back, and we can't do anything but to miss them today, and hope that they can happen again someday—even if we know there is no chance at all.

I Still Love You

I still love you

like you've never hurt me.

I still love you

like I never felt the pain.

I still love you

like you're still mine.

I still love you

like I always do.

Pairs

There are things that work in pairs. For instance, a pen and a paper. I want us to be like them. A pen is useless without a paper and vice versa.

I want to be the pen that writes thoughts and feelings. You will be the paper where I will write in.

We could have worked as a pair, but you already have something written in your pages.

We would have been a pair, but you already have a pen who writes on you.

Sing You a Song

I want to sing you a song

but I am afraid that

all I could do

is sob.

Promise

We both know that nothing is certain. If there is something that is constant, it's change. We can walk away from reality, but we can never hide from it.

But I want you to know that no matter how long, I want our love to remain the same.

I love you today. I don't want to change what I feel for you now.

I will love you tomorrow and the day after tomorrow. I don't want to be with someone if that someone is not you.

I will love you forever. And that's a promise.

I Love You

I love you

and it's enough reason

to make me believe that

it's all worth the pain.

Why?

Why, why, why? When someone you truly love leaves you, you will keep on asking that question—as if there was never an answer.

Love Back

You made me know

how it feels like to love.

You made me curious

how it feels like to be loved back.

Never a Poet

I was never a poet, until you left me.

Enough

Enough

thinking of the past

and wishing that

we can go back.

Enough

looking for you

because you're already

settled down with him.

Enough

hurting myself

by hoping that

you'll be coming back.

My Goodbye

I just want to tell you before I wave goodbye, that you still have a huge space in my heart.

Everybody may lie to you. But I promise you I am saying the truth every time I say 'I love you'.

He may hurt you, but I can never do that.

The whole world may turn its back on you, but I am just here. If ever you want to come back to me, do not hesitate. You're always welcome, no matter what happens.

I love you. I always do. And I always will.

Goodbye, for now.

Before and Now

Forgive me

for loving you before

for still loving you now

for I can't stop loving you

even if you're married now.

ABOUT THE AUTHOR

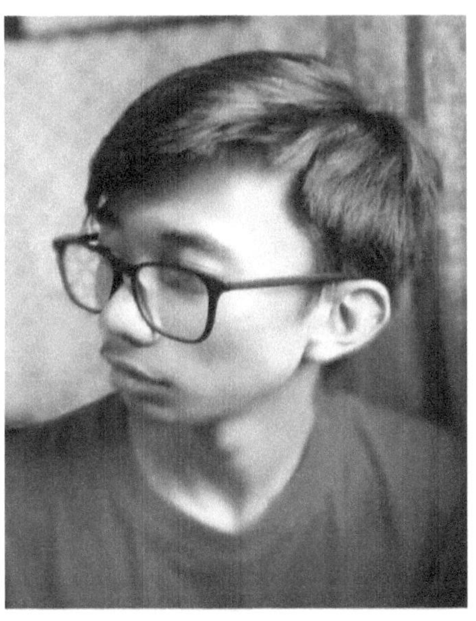

Harold Patrick Mercado is a college student taking up Bachelor of Secondary Education in English major at Polytechnic University of the Philippines in Maragondon, Cavite. He was the editor-in-chief of their campus publication during his senior high school stay at Doyong National High School in San Carlos City, Pangasinan. Writing poetry is something he always looks forward to every day. It is his passion since childhood. He believes that what makes a great art is the heart.

Follow Patrick:

Facebook:

facebook.com/haroldpatrick.mercado

Facebook Page:

facebook.com/AuthorHaroldPatrick/

Instagram:

instagram.com/iampatrickmercado

YouTube:

https://www.youtube.com/channel/UC8h4Lzs4Mlh-
CAARGaD-aew